YORUBALAND

THE KINGDOMS OF AFRICA

YORUBALAND

THE FLOWERING OF GENIUS

PHILIP KOSLOW

CHELSEA HOUSE PUBLISHERS • New York • Philadelphia

Frontispiece: A 19th-century engraving depicts a group of travelers making their way through a dense tropical forest in Yorubaland.

On the Cover: An artist's interpretation of a bronze head from Ife, the spiritual center of Yorubaland; in the background, the entrance to a Yoruba village.

CHELSEA HOUSE PUBLISHERS
Editorial Director Richard Rennert
Executive Managing Editor Karyn Gullen Browne
Copy Chief Robin James
Picture Editor Adrian G. Allen
Creative Director Robert Mitchell
Art Director Joan Ferrigno
Production Manager Sallye Scott

THE KINGDOMS OF AFRICA
Senior Editor Martin Schwabacher

Staff for YORUBALAND
Assistant Editor Catherine Iannone
Editorial Assistant Erin McKenna
Designer Cambraia Magalhães
Picture Researcher Lisa Kirchner
Cover Illustrator Bradford Brown

First Printing
1 3 5 7 9 8 6 4 2

Library of Congress Cataloging-in-Publication Data

Koslow, Philip.
  Yorubaland: the flowering of genius/ Philip Koslow.
    p. cm.—(The Kingdoms of Africa)
Includes bibliographical references and index.
  ISBN   0-7910-3131-4.
            0-7910-3132-2 (pbk.)
  1. Yoruba (African people)—History—Juvenile literature. [1. Yoruba (African people)] I. Title. II.
Series.   95-5974
DT515.45Y67 1995   CIP
960'.049633—dc20   AC

CONTENTS

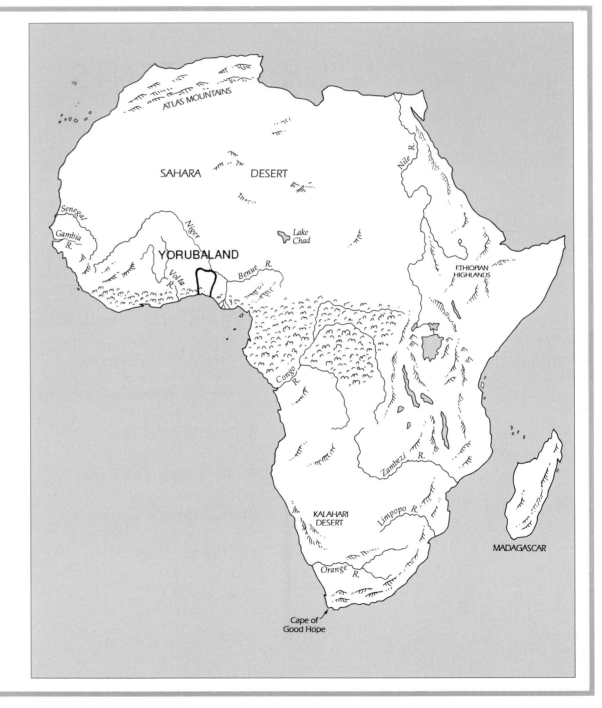

"CIVILIZATION AND MAGNIFICENCE"

On a sunny morning in July 1796, Mungo Park, a Scottish doctor turned explorer, achieved a major goal of his long and difficult trek through West Africa when he reached the banks of the mighty Niger River. Along the river was a cluster of four large towns, which together made up the city of Segu, the principal settlement of the Bambara people. The sight of Segu dazzled Park as much as the spectacle of the broad, shining waterway. "The view of this extensive city," he wrote, "the numerous canoes upon the river; the crowded population; and the cultivated state of the surrounding country, formed altogether a prospect of civilization and magnificence, which I little expected to find in the bosom of Africa."

Park's account of his journey, *Travels in the Interior Districts of Africa*, became a best-seller in England. But his positive reflections on Africa were soon brushed aside by the English and other Europeans, who were engaged in a profitable trade in slaves along the West African coast and were eventually to carve up the entire continent into colonies. Later explorers such as Richard Burton, who spoke of the "childishness" and "backwardness" of Africans, achieved more lasting fame than did Park, who drowned during a second expedition to Africa in 1806. Thus it is not surprising that 100 years after Park's arrival at Segu, a professor at England's Oxford University could write with bland self-assurance that African history before the arrival of Europeans had been nothing more than "blank, uninteresting, brutal barbarism." The professor's opinion was published when the British Empire was at its height, and it represented a point of view that was necessary to justify the exploitation of Africans. If, as the professor claimed, Africans had lived in a state of chaos throughout their history, then their European conquerors

7

A relief map of Africa indicating the territory of Yorubaland.

8

8

A sculpture depicting chi wara (a legendary being who was half human and half antelope) created by the Bambara people of West Africa, who achieved a high level of political organization during the 18th century.

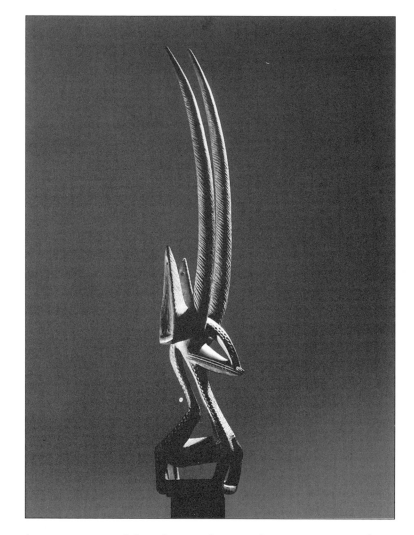

could believe that they were doing a noble deed by imposing their will and their way of life upon Africa.

The colonialist view of African history held sway into the 20th century. But as the century progressed, more enlightened scholars began to take a fresh look at the African past. As archaeologists (scientists who study the physical remains of past societies) explored the sites of former African cities, they found that Africans had enjoyed a high level of civilization hundreds of years before the arrival of Europeans. In many respects, the kingdoms and cities of Africa had been equal to or more advanced than European societies during the same period.

Modern scientists also reject the idea—fostered by Europeans during the time of the slave trade and colonialism— that there is any connection between a people's skin color and its capacity for achievement and self-government. Differences in pigmentation, scientists now recognize, are based solely upon climate and have nothing to do with intellectual ability. When the human species began to develop in the torrid regions of Africa some 7.5 million years ago, humans were all dark skinned because dark pigmentation protected them from the harmful ultraviolet rays of the sun.

However, for those people who later migrated from Africa to colder climates where there was far less sunlight, heavy pigmentation became a drawback—it prevented the skin from absorbing the amount of sunlight needed to produce vitamin D, which is essential for the growth of bones and teeth. Hence lighter skin began to predominate in Europe, with the peoples of Asia, the Middle East, and North Africa occupying a middle ground between Europeans and dark-skinned Africans. Rather than indicating superiority, therefore, lighter skin can be viewed as a divergence from the original skin color of all human beings.

As early as the 5th century B.C., when ancient Greece was enjoying its Golden Age, West African peoples had also developed a highly civilized way of life and were producing magnificent works of art. By A.D. 750, ancient Ghana, known as the Land of Gold, emerged as West Africa's first centralized kingdom. When Ghana began to decline in the 12th century, power shifted to the empire of Mali, and Mali was in turn supplanted by Songhay, Kanem-Borno, and the fortress kingdoms of Hausaland. All these great nations were located in the central part of West Africa, a wide, sun-baked savanna that borders the vast Sahara Desert. To a large extent, they owed their wealth and grandeur to trade with North Africa and the Middle East. Because of this ever-widening economic and cultural contact, the fame of the Bilad al-Sudan ("land of the black peoples" in Arabic) spread throughout the world.

However, the rich saga of the savanna states does not represent the entire history of West African achievement. Indeed, much of the savanna's wealth derived from the gold, ivory, and kola nuts produced by the peoples of the lush forest belt that extends from the Atlantic coast of West Africa to the Gulf of Guinea. The forestland communities had emerged at least as early as those of the savanna, but their location and terrain ensured that they would be largely unknown to outsiders until the arrival of European mariners in the 15th century. Their history forms a unique chapter in the development of African civilization, and some of the most remarkable contributions to that civilization were made by the people of Yorubaland.

Chapter **1** | # THE CHILDREN OF ODUDUWA

An aerial view of the rain forest that blankets the West African coast. Throughout much of their history, the Yoruba and other peoples of the forest belt were shielded from outsiders by the rugged terrain of their homeland.

The West African forest has always presented a formidable and often frightening barrier to outsiders. Even the early North African traders, a hardy, adventurous group of men who regularly braved the two-month-long journey across the Sahara Desert to reach the cities of the Sudan, did not venture into the forest belt but chose instead to trade through middlemen. A 19th-century European traveler, quoted by Graham Connah in his book *African Civilizations*, provided a graphic description of the daunting challenges presented by the forest landscape:

> The doom and iron-wood trees were frequent; the path was a labyrinth of the most capricious windings, the roots of the cotton trees obstructing it continually. . . . Immense trunks of fallen trees presented constant barriers to our progress, and increased our fatigues from the labor of scaling them. . . . The large trees were covered by parasites and convulvuli, and the climbing plants, like small cables, ascending the trunks to some height, abruptly shot downwards, crossed to the opposite trees, and threaded each other in such a perplexity of twists and turnings, that it soon became impossible to trace them in the general entanglement.

Such natural barriers did not deter the ancestors of the Yoruba. Numerous traditions recount the origin of the Yoruba and their communities. According to one tradition, both the Yoruba and the rest of the human race derived from Olodumare, the supreme being. Olodumare sent his agent, Oduduwa, down to earth and charged him with creating land upon the waters. Oduduwa descended from heaven on a chain, accompanied by a five-toed chicken, and came to Ile Ife, the spiritual center of the Yoruba people. (In Yoruba, *ile* means "homeland.") After Oduduwa sprinkled sand upon the waters, the chicken scattered the sand with its feet, thus creating the land the Yoruba were to dwell on. Then Oduduwa created human beings out of clay, and Olodumare breathed life into them. The people later dispersed throughout Yorubaland and, led by 16 companions who had followed Oduduwa out of heaven, established the various Yoruba settlements.

A second tradition maintains that Oduduwa was the son of a king who lived in the East, in the city of Mecca. Mecca is the holy city of Islam, one of the world's great religions, and Oduduwa's father was a staunch Muslim, or follower of Islam. Oduduwa rebelled against his father by worshiping the idols of traditional gods rather than Allah, the god of the Muslim religion. The rebellious prince attracted many followers, and finally a civil war broke out between the Muslims and the idol worshipers. In the end, Oduduwa and his allies were forced to flee from Mecca. They journeyed to Ile Ife, where they set up their idols in a sacred forest grove, and from there they expanded into the rest of Yorubaland.

At first glance, the two traditions might appear to clash, as one version claims that Oduduwa was a god and the other presents him as a person of flesh and blood. But they are actually separate parts of the same story. The first tradition commemorates the arrival of the Yoruba in the forestlands, and the second confirms the advent of the rulers who governed them through the most glorious epoch of their history.

Scholars have determined that the Yoruba first occupied their present territory (which covers about 70,000 square miles to the west of the lower branch of the Niger River) at least as early as the 4th century A.D. Prior to that time, large-scale settlement in the forest belt was nearly impossible: the tools employed by people in that region were all made of stone and bone and were incapable of felling large trees or clearing dense underbrush. Gradually, Africans learned to extract iron from chunks of stone and to fashion the metal into tools and weapons. They were then able to expand into regions that had once been remote and forbidding.

Like most black Africans, the Yoruba practiced a religion that paid homage to

12

the spirits dwelling in the earth. They believed that if the spirits did not accept their presence, disaster would follow—the rains would not fall, the crops would not grow, the waters would not yield fish, the hunters would kill no animals. By identifying Oduduwa, the son of the supreme being, as the founder of their communities, the Yoruba boldly restated their right to occupy the land and also reinforced the sacred bond between the people and the earth. When future generations recited these traditions, they would renew their claim to Yorubaland and remember their obligation to the gods of their ancestors.

With their iron-bladed axes, machetes, and hoes, the Yoruba settlers cleared large tracts of forestland and planted crops. The staple of their diet was the yam. Successful yam farming was a challenging and sometimes backbreaking job. The seeds were planted after the first rains, usually in midsummer, and throughout the next three months they had to be carefully tended as their green leaves sprouted above the surface and their thick roots grew steadily in the earth. During the growing season, farmers would often work their fields from sunup to sundown, hoping for the right combination of sunlight and rain: too

13

A terra-cotta sculpture depicting an early Yoruba ruler. According to Yoruba tradition, Oranmiyan—the son of Oduduwa and the grandson of Olodumare—went forth from Ife to conquer neighboring peoples and found new Yoruba communities.

14

An engraving of the entrance to a Yoruba village. Throughout their history, the Yoruba have sustained themselves by growing yams and other crops; rather than living on their farms, however, they settled in highly organized communities surrounded by protective walls.

much heat would wither the young plants, and too much rain would wash away the soil and stunt the roots. Finally, as the crops reached maturity, the entire community would celebrate. The Nigerian novelist Chinua Achebe has described the importance of this moment among the Yoruba's neighbors to the east, the Igbo:

> The Feast of the New Yam was held every year before the harvest began, to honor the earth goddess and the ancestral spirits of the clan. New yams could not be eaten until some had first been offered to these powers. Men and women, young and old, looked forward to the New Yam Festival because it began the season of plenty—the new year. On the last night before the festival, yams of the old year were all disposed of by those who still had them. . . . All cooking pots, calabashes and wooden bowls were thoroughly washed, especially the wooden mortar in which the yam was pounded. Yam foo-foo and vegetable soup was the chief food in the celebration. So much of it was cooked that, no matter how heavily the family ate or how many friends and relatives they invited from neighboring villages, there was always a large quantity of food left over at the end of the day.

In addition to yams, the Yoruba cultivated the oil palm, a tree whose seeds and fruit yield a nutritious and flavorful oil, and they harvested kola nuts, which contain a substance similar to caffeine and are highly valued for their properties as stimulants and thirst quenchers. The Yoruba were not only able to sustain themselves with these crops but could also build up surpluses. They then traded with the savanna states and supplemented their diet with such foods as sorghum, millet, and rice.

As they increased in number, the Yoruba began to live in villages surrounded by earthen walls, within walking distance of their farms. Village life had a powerful impact on the social system of the Yoruba. Most basically, the Yoruba organized themselves around clans or descent lines: families sharing a common ancestor lived side by side in extended compounds. Each compound was headed by an elder known as the *bale* or *oloro ebi.* With the expansion of agriculture and trade, it became desirable for people possessing similar skills— whether as farmers, tool makers, traders, or warriors—to live close together. Villages, therefore, began to be organized according to profession as well as along descent lines. It was also convenient to have certain individuals assume command of various activities, especially war and trade. By A.D. 600, chiefs and kings began to appear among the Yoruba.

Scholars believe that the traditions depicting Oduduwa as a prince from Mecca, along with archaeological evidence, point to the later arrival of a conquering group that replaced the original Yoruba rulers. In the opinion of Roland Oliver and Brian Fagan, these conquerors came from the northwest, probably Hausaland, around 1300. Their original language was probably Kanuri or Hausa, but they soon married Yoruba women, and their children grew up speaking Yoruba. In religious terms, the newcomers would have had no trouble fitting in. Oliver and Fagan believe that the conquerors left their homeland because they upheld the traditional religions against Islam, which was rapidly penetrating the Sudan and gaining influence among West African rulers. (Thus the "Mecca" of the Oduduwa legend represents Islam rather than a geographic location.) Because they defended the traditional religion and suffered exile for their faith, the children of Oduduwa would not be seen merely as foreign intruders. On the contrary, both their military strength and their religious principles made them ideal guardians for the sacred groves of Ife, where the ancestral gods of the Yoruba resided. In these groves arose one of the glories of world civilization.

Chapter 2 | THE SACRED CENTER

A pair of brass figures (one male and one female) carried by members of the Ogboni Society, a Yoruba religious organization that punishes offenses against the earth. Like other African peoples, the Yoruba strive to achieve harmony with the spirits of the natural world.

In Yoruba belief the supreme being, Olodumare, also known as Olorun ("owner of the sky"), creates each human soul. However, he does not involve himself in everyday human affairs. This task is the province of the gods known as *orisa*. Yoruba religion accounts for more than 400 orisa. Some are worshiped only by a particular descent line or by the residents of a particular locality; others are worshiped throughout Yorubaland.

Among the most important of the universal gods is Orishanla, the brother of Oduduwa. According to some traditions, Orishanla took over the task of creating human beings when Oduduwa became drunk on palm wine. Orishanla, described in Yoruba praise songs as "one who creates a person as he chooses," is responsible for the existence of albinos,

hunchbacks, dwarfs, and those who lack the power to walk or speak—all these individuals are considered sacred beings by the Yoruba.

A god who has played a significant role in Yoruba history is Ogun, who is said to have cleared a path for the other orisa when they descended to earth. Ogun is associated with the forging of iron and the making of weapons and tools. He is therefore both a war god and the god of blacksmiths, who—because of the power conferred by iron—are highly respected and sometimes feared in many West African societies. Related to Ogun is Oshoshi, the god of the hunt, whose symbols are a bow and arrows.

Shango, the god of thunder, hurls thunderstones to the earth, killing those who offend him. When farmers find these stones (about the size of ax heads) in their fields, they take them to Shango's shrine and make offerings to him. Another troublesome god is Eshu (also known as Elegba), the youngest and cleverest of the orisa. Eshu serves as the messenger of the gods, but he also plays tricks on his fellow orisa and brings misfortune to human beings who do not worship in the proper way. During the 19th century, Christian and Muslim missionaries among the Yoruba often identified Eshu with Satan, though modern schol-

A Yoruba priest, or babalawo, *performing* Ifa *divination. Yoruba men and women commonly consult a* babalawo *to learn about their individual destinies or to seek guidance in making important decisions.*

ars recognize that Eshu is far more to the Yoruba than a mere symbol of evil. Indeed, the figure of Eshu expresses the complexity of the Yoruba worldview and their belief that individuals control their own fate. When people do not behave properly, Eshu unleashes the evil forces (ajogun) in the universe, and the resulting punishment can be devastating. However, those who follow the right path in life can rely on Eshu to activate the good ajogun in their favor, and thus they will reap enormous rewards.

The Yoruba also honor a host of female deities. Among them are Oshun, a beautiful goddess with many lovers among the orisa, who is credited with the power to cause the conception of children; Yemoja, goddess of the river Ogun; and Olokun, the sea goddess. One of the most powerful goddesses is Oya, the wife of Shango, called "the wife who is fiercer than the husband." As William Bascom has written in *16 Cowries,* a study of Yoruba worship, "When Shango wishes to fight with lightning, he sends his wife ahead of him to fight with wind. She blows roofs off houses, knocks down large trees, and fans the fires set by Shango's thunderbolts into a high blaze."

Though Yoruba traditions vary substantially from region to region, they all agree that the orisa are intimately involved in the personal life of each Yoruba and in the development of Yoruba history. The traditions name various orisa as the first rulers of the Yoruba states, and Yoruba religion teaches that each person is under the care of a particular orisa.

In order to comprehend the relations between individuals and the gods, the

The face carved into this wooden divining board is believed to represent Eshu, the messenger between the Yoruba and their gods. The babalawo uses the board, some divining powder, and 16 palm nuts to select religious verses that relate to the situation of the person seeking guidance.

20

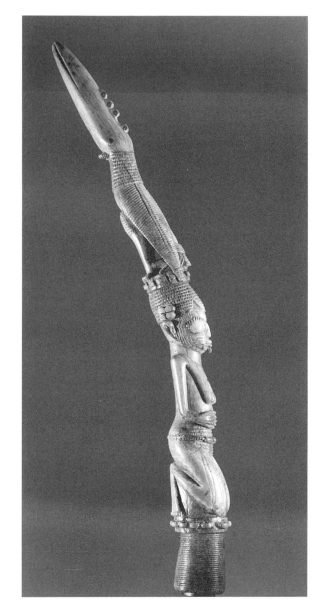

A wand employed in Ifa divination for the purpose of drawing the attention of the gods. The ancient Yoruba divination rites have survived intact for centuries and are now employed throughout the Americas as well as in Africa.

Yoruba developed an elaborate system of mediation. The most immediate agent of mediation is the head of a family, who is responsible for communicating with ancestors. Like many West African peoples, the Yoruba believe that the souls of their ancestors remain in close contact with the earth and will be reborn in future generations. (Distinctively, though, the Yoruba conceive of a "good heaven" and a "bad heaven" and believe that souls assigned to the bad heaven may never return to earth.) As E. Thomas Lawson writes in his 1984 book *The Religions of Africa*, the head of the family "represents the people to the ancestors by sacrificing to the ancestors on behalf of the people, and he represents the ancestors to the people by informing the family members of their obligations to the ancestors."

On a community level, the Yoruba communicate with the orisa at the sacred shrines. At each shrine, the worshiper is assisted by a priest known as a *babalawo* ("father of secret things" in the Yoruba language). Worshipers go to the shrines with the purpose of understanding their destiny, which the soul chooses when it is created by Olodumare but which is then forgotten by a person in the actual process of birth. The babalawo helps the supplicant recall his or her destiny by communicating with Ifa, the god of divination.

Lawson has described the basic divination process in the following terms:

> The elements are sixteen palm nuts, . . . a divining board, and divining powder [in past times, yam flour or powdered camwood]. . . . [The priest] will place the sixteen nuts in his left hand and then attempt to take as many of them with his right hand as possible. If only one nut remains, then he will make a double mark in the divining powder on the divining board. If two nuts remain, he will make a single mark. If no nuts or more than two remain, he will make no marks. The purpose is to end with two columns with four sets of two marks in each column. . . . There are 256 possible combinations of such marks. Each of these sets of marks has a traditional story associated with it. The babalawo will know at least four such parables, or Odu, for each of these 256 sets. . . . When a particular set has been arrived at by the diviner and the appropriate story has been chosen, he will inform the consulter which action the story recommends be performed.

William Bascom, who studied Yoruba religion for many years, points out that Ifa divination is even more complex than the Chinese system of I Ching, which has long been popular in the West. The I Ching contains only 8 basic figures and 64 derivative figures, compared to Ifa's 16 and 256. This complexity is a testament to the richness of Yoruba religion and culture. In his book *Ifa Divination*, Bascom writes:

> The real core of Ifa divination lies in the thousands of memorized verses by means of which the 256 figures are interpreted. . . . These verses are of far greater importance than either the figures themselves or the manipulations from which they are derived. The verses form an important corpus of verbal art, including myths, folktales, praise names, incantations, songs, proverbs, and even riddles; but to the Yoruba their "literary" merit is second to their religious significance. In effect these verses constitute their unwritten scripture.

The culture that elaborated this rich oral literature produced at the same time some of the greatest artworks the world has ever seen.

Chapter 3 | THE FLOWERING OF GENIUS

A bronze statue of an oni—showing the ruler's traditional crown, collar, and beads—from the Wunmonije Grove in Ife. Statues such as this one were commonly used in funeral ceremonies and then displayed in shrines; Yoruba rulers would visit the shrines and pay homage to the spirits of their predecessors.

In 1910, when Yorubaland was part of the British colony of Nigeria, the ruler of Ife permitted a German anthropologist named Leo Frobenius to visit one of the sacred groves outside the city. As Frobenius wrote in his account of the expedition:

> We reached the bush and forest country after some time, and, branching off the main road, which tended Southwestwards, our leader took us, now dryshod and now in the bed of an old tributary stream, beneath a wonderful avenue of overhanging palms. A venerable old man, the owner of the sacred relics, came out to meet us. . . . The ancient man approached and pointed everything out; he explained the avenue of palms and related the story of the great Shango's journey, which the God made through an old tree (whose giant trunk had been seared by lightning). . . . While all this was going on, Martius and myself happened upon . . . one or two bits of reddish terra-cotta embedded in the earth. . . . They were pieces of a broken human face. . . . Here were the remains of a very ancient and fine type of art. . . . These meager relics were eloquent of a symmetry, a vitality, a delicacy of form directly reminiscent of ancient Greece.

Sharing the widespread European belief in the "backwardness" of Africans, Frobenius believed that these ancient sculptures must have been European in origin. He theorized that the ancient Greeks had once established a colony, the mythical realm of Atlantis, on the coast of West Africa and that the Ife sculptures were remnants of that civili-

24

zation. Most scholars of the day rejected Frobenius's claim to have discovered Atlantis, but they shared his cultural bias. No one was prepared to accept the possibility that such magnificent works had been created by African artists: thus the theory arose that the sculptures of Ife—and every other achievement of black Africa—were the legacy of the Hamites, a light-skinned race of North Africans who had once dominated the darker-skinned peoples of the interior.

By the latter part of the 20th century, both Frobenius's ideas and the various Hamitic theories had been totally rejected by scholars studying the African past. No reputable scholar now doubts that black Africans created the great works of Ife. As the historian Robert Smith has noted in his 1988 book *Kingdoms of the Yoruba*:

> The facial characteristics of most of the sculptures are undoubtedly negroid, and indeed striking similarities to the modern inhabitants of Ife can sometimes be detected, as well as family resemblances between different groups of the sculptures. The striations, or skin scarifications, which appear prominently on some of the faces, and in the large bronze figures on the abdomen, probably represent tribal marks. . . . Moreover, since attention was first drawn to the antiq-

uities of Ife, finds have continued apace, and excavations in and around the town produce a flow of objects. Thus it is reasonable to assume that these antiquities were the product of a civilization in Ife itself which was ancestral to the present culture of the Yoruba, and that both the artists and their human subjects were the ancestors of the Ife of the present day.

Employing modern methods of dating artifacts, scholars have concluded that the terra-cotta figures of Ife date from the 12th through the 14th centuries and that the bronze figures date from the 14th to the 15th centuries. The terra-cottas show evidence of strong links with the sculptures produced by the Nok culture, which flourished directly to the north of Yorubaland. Though the Nok culture died out long ago and its latest surviving artworks have been dated only to the year 200, the techniques of firing terra-cotta could easily have survived in the region until a new cultural awakening brought them into play.

The art of Ife is not a mere continuation of the art of Nok, however. For one thing, many of the Ife artworks are naturalistic. That is, they attempt to reproduce the human figure in exact detail. By contrast, the art of Nok and of most other African cultures throughout the ages has

(Continued on page 29)

THE ART OF IFE

Ife, located in the southern part of present-day Nigeria, has been the spiritual center of the Yoruba nation for hundreds of years. Between the 12th and 16th centuries, the artists of Ife produced numerous sculptures that rank among the world's greatest artworks.

This lifelike head from Ife is sculpted in terra-cotta, a form of clay that becomes exceptionally hard when heated in a fire. Art historians have advanced different theories to explain the facial striations on many of the Ife heads; some believe the markings represent tribal affiliations, while others suggest they may designate different branches of Ife's royal family.

26

This bronze statue of an oni, the traditional ruler of Ife, *dates from the 14th or 15th century. The sculpture includes many symbols of the oni's office, including the ram's horn and scepter in his hands, the beaded crown and collar, and the long necklace that extends down to his waist.*

Though apparently created in Ife, this exquisite copper sculpture came into the possession of the Nupe, the Yoruba's eastern neighbors. Nupe traditions claim that the statue was taken from Yorubaland in the 16th century by Tsoede, a legendary hero credited with founding Nupe's ruling dynasty.

A bronze head from Ife, possibly representing the sea god, Olokun. Some of the greatest Ife sculptures were unearthed during the early 20th century in a sacred forest grove dedicated to the worship of Olokun.

(Continued from page 24)

portrayed both humans and animals in broad outline, striving for dramatic form and emotional impact rather than trying to mirror reality. (For this reason, the 20th-century European masters who created what is now called modern art, such as Pablo Picasso, drew upon African art to create their visually and emotionally powerful works.) Some scholars have speculated that there may have been a religious principle in many African societies that forbade the exact portrayal of a subject. For a time, at least, this taboo did not operate in Ife, allowing the artists to create lifelike (and life-size) heads.

In addition to creating innovations in style, the later Ife artists also worked in bronze, a material unknown to the creators of Nok. Bronze is an alloy (a combination of metals) made up mostly of copper, and deposits of copper ore do not exist in Yorubaland or surrounding areas. For this reason, bronze casting was not possible in Yorubaland until copper mined in North Africa made its way southward along the trade routes of the Sahara and Sudan. Needless to say, Yoruba artists would have had no interest in acquiring copper unless they had been taught how to use it. The advent of both copper and casting skills in the 14th century fits neatly with Yoruba traditions

The artists of Ife began to sculpt terra-cotta heads such as this one during the 12th century. Though these works continue an artistic tradition begun centuries earlier in Nok, their expressiveness and detail are unmatched by any previous African artworks.

29

about the migration from "Mecca." Clearly, the northern immigrants who began to dominate Yorubaland at this time had mastered the various technologies that had developed among the African peoples of the Nile Valley and spread gradually into North Africa and the Sudan.

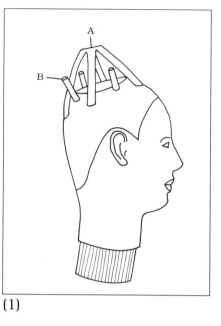

(1)

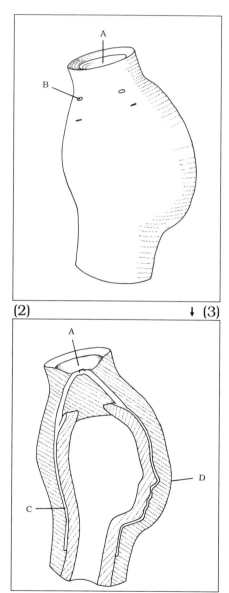

(2)   ↓ (3)

30

This series of drawings illustrate the essential steps in the lost-wax method of bronze casting. Figure (1) shows the wax model with tubes (A) for pouring molten bronze and vents (B) to allow the escape of heated air. Figure (2) shows the outer clay mold in place. Figure (3) is a cross-section of the sculpture: molten bronze will fill the space (C) that remains after the wax has melted off, and the outer mold (D) will be removed after the bronze has cooled and set.

The artist would first make a clay model of the sculpture. When the clay dried, he would apply a thin layer of beeswax and carefully etch all the details of the sculpture into the wax. Then he would cover the wax with several more layers of clay, forming a thick mold. When the entire form was heated over a fire, the middle layer of wax would melt and drain off through the bottom of the form. At this point, the sculptor poured molten bronze into the top of the mold through a series of tubes. The bronze filled the space where the "lost" wax had been, conforming to all the fine details now baked into surrounding clay. When the bronze cooled and set, the outer layers of clay were carefully broken, and the finished sculpture emerged.

The lifelike heads of Ife may be the memorial portraits of kings. Because the dead had to be buried quickly in the warm, humid climate of Yorubaland, there was no time for elaborate funeral ceremonies centering on the body of the monarch. Therefore, the artists would make an impression of the head and create a life-size sculpture that could represent the king at a later ceremony. During the funeral rites, the head would be mounted atop a wooden sculpture on which the royal robes and other kingly symbols were represented. When the mourners had concluded all their observances, they would bury the head in one of the sacred groves.

Whatever the ultimate meaning of the Ife sculptures, the sophistication behind them is clear. As Robert Smith has written: "The inspiration and aesthetic judgment which enabled the artists to create their sculpture must have been rooted in a culture of distinction and maturity, which in turn could only have evolved against a background of a sufficient political stability. . . . These artists and craftsmen, from the quality of their work, must have been professionals whose activities were only possible in a society where economic life had attained a high degree of organization and differentiation."

In the case of Ife, records of that political and economic organization are sketchy. To understand these aspects of Yoruba achievement, students must turn instead to the saga of Yorubaland's most powerful state.

A finished bronze mask from Ife, said to represent Obalufon II, the ruler who introduced the art of bronze casting. The holes around the head and face allow the fitting of a crown and a beard—these decorations were most likely connected with particular ceremonies.

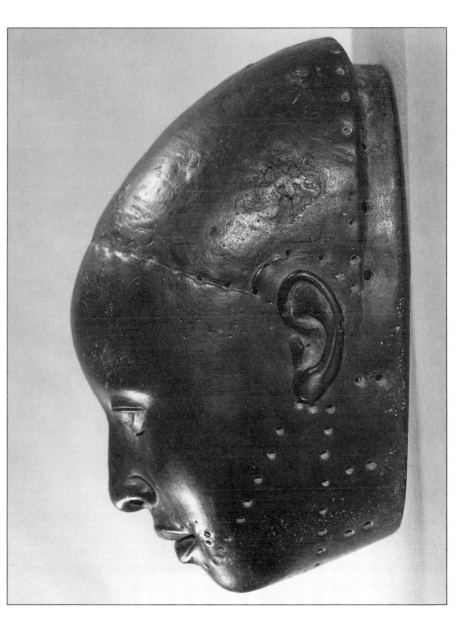

Chapter 4 | THE HIGHLANDS EMPIRE

An engraving of West African cavalry in action. In the late 16th century, when the alafins became wealthy enough to import horses and build up their mounted armies, Oyo quickly began to emerge as the dominant state in Yorubaland.

Nestled in the dense rain forest, Ife represents only one physical aspect of Yorubaland. As a traveler proceeds northward from the coast toward the Niger and the site of Oyo Ile (Old Oyo), the elevation of the land increases and the forest begins to thin out. Emerging from the dense, misty woodlands, the traveler enters a broad savanna where outcrops of greenery and rocky hills dot the rolling, tawny terrain.

According to Yoruba tradition, the journey from the coast to the highlands was first made by Oranmiyan, one of Oduduwa's grandsons. Oranmiyan set out with a powerful army to avenge the expulsion of his grandfather from "Mecca," and in the midst of his conquests he founded Oyo Ile. To this day, a tall stone obelisk, known as the Staff of Oranmiyan, marks the site of his grave.

Throughout most of its history, Oyo was no different in status from the other Yoruba states, which included (in addition to Ife) Ekiti, Egbado, Ijebu, Ketu, Nago, Ondo, Owo, and Igbomina. Each state was governed by a king who bore a distinctive title: *oni* in Ife, *alafin* in Oyo, *olowo* in Owo, and *ewi* in Ado, to name a few. All the monarchs were considered descendants of Oduduwa, entitled to wear Oduduwa's crown, which is adorned with a beaded fringe. Similarly, all the states were supposed to be equal partners in the Yoruba's *ebi* ("family") system of government. Nevertheless, because of Ife's central role in Yoruba tradition, the oni of Ife had always served as the spiritual leader of all the Yoruba. And by the 16th century, Oyo and its alafins began to emerge as the most powerful political force in Yorubaland.

Thanks to Oranmiyan's conquests, Oyo was the largest of the Yoruba states, and this certainly contributed to its growing status. Geography and climate played equally important roles. For one thing, Oyo possessed especially fertile soil: abundant food production made it possible for Oyo's population to grow and provided large surpluses for trade. Equally important, Oyo's access to the Niger River afforded easy communication with the wealthy trading cities of the Songhay empire—principally Gao, Timbuktu, and Jenne—situated on the western branch of the great waterway. Its location in the savanna did leave Oyo more vulnerable to attack than Ife and the other forest states, but Oyo also possessed a unique ability to build up its military forces.

Living in the forest belt, most of the Yoruba could not keep horses because of the tsetse fly. One of Africa's most dangerous pests, the tsetse transmits a deadly parasitic disease, commonly known as sleeping sickness, to both humans and animals. However, the tsetse does not breed successfully in the drier, more open country of the savanna. Because of this advantage, a number of the West African savanna states had been able to create large cavalry forces that enabled them to dominate their neighbors and build powerful empires.

Oyo was not far enough from the forest belt to allow the breeding of horses large enough for use as cavalry mounts. However, the sturdy North African and Arabian breeds could survive for a year or two in Oyo, long enough to be serviceable in war. The Oyo well understood the importance of cavalry because they endured numerous raids from their northern neighbors, particularly Nupe and Borgu.

Toward the end of the 16th century, the Oyo had amassed sufficient wealth from trade to import large numbers of horses, dealing mainly through the fa-

34

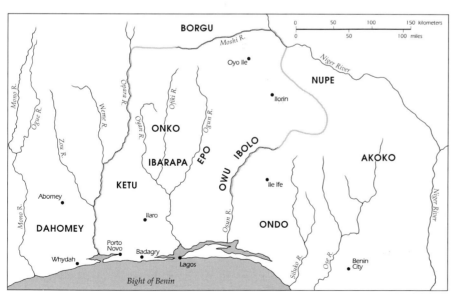

A map of Yorubaland, showing the Oyo empire at the height of its power.

mous traders of Hausaland. Orompoto, the 10th alafin, is credited with transforming Oyo's mounted forces into a formidable fighting machine. According to tradition, Orompoto devised the technique of tying leaves to the tails of the cavalry mounts: the leaves would sweep the ground behind the horses, erasing their hoofprints and mystifying enemies trying to locate the Oyo forces.

The principal weapons of the Oyo armies were the sword and the spear, all locally manufactured out of iron. One popular variety of sword, known as the *ida*, was double-edged and could be either straight or slightly curved. A second type, the *agedengbe*, is described by Robert Smith as having "a broad single-edged iron blade curving backwards, which . . . would have great shearing force. . . . The types [of sword] seen by the writer, many of which would be useless for thrusting, suggest . . . that among the Yoruba the sword was regarded essentially as a cutting weapon."

Spears were usually of two varieties: the *oko*, a thrusting spear, and the *esin*, a throwing spear or javelin. The oko, consisting of a wooden shaft and an iron head, could range from about six to eight feet in length; the esin was lighter, somewhat shorter, and consequently better balanced. As Smith has indicated, "The weapon was usually carried by the warrior, when charging on foot or on horseback, under the right arm with the left hand supporting it about half-way down the shaft." Smith goes on to point out that spearheads were frequently poisoned: "A concoction would be made from various leaves and roots . . . to which the crushed heads of snakes were added. The spears were dipped into this brew before being taken into battle, and informants claimed that wounds inflicted

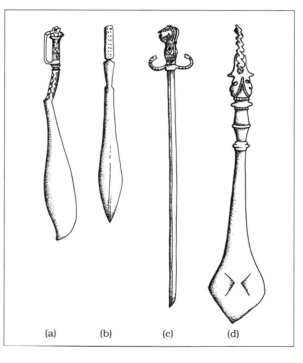

(a)   (b)   (c)   (d)

The Yoruba manufactured their own iron swords, following a number of different designs. Sword (a) is an agedengbe; (b) and (c) are of the ida type; and (d) is a type of sword used only for ceremonial purposes.

by the poisoned points sometimes caused instantaneous death. The efficacy of the poison on the iron heads is said to last for many years." Yoruba soldiers also used the bow and arrow (said to be capable of killing an elephant at close range), clubs, axes, throwing knives, and spiked iron bracelets, which were employed in hand-to-hand fighting.

Unlike the cavalry of the Hausa states and Kanem-Borno, the Yoruba horsemen did not wear body armor in battle. Most soldiers wore padded jackets decorated with cowries (small white shells often used as money in West Africa) and various charms designed to prevent wounds; leaders often wore a garment called the *wabi*, or war apron. Yoruba armies did not adopt any sort of uniform. At close range, friend could be distinguished from foe by the tribal marks etched into the cheeks of the warriors.

Once they had secured their borders, the Oyo went on the offensive and turned the tables on their former assailants. During the 17th century, such leaders as the alafins Obalokun and Ajagbo rebuilt Oyo Ile and began to create an empire. First they conquered Sabe and Ketu, their neighbors to the southwest. Then they gradually took control of the territory on both sides of the Ogun River until

they reached the coast. In this way, the Oyo gained control of all traffic on the river and secured the city of Ajase (also known as Porto Novo), from which they could trade with the European merchants who had been plying the coast of Africa since the 15th century.

On the whole, the purpose of warfare in West Africa was not the actual conquest of territory. West African rulers were more interested in taking prisoners who could be employed as servants, soldiers, and laborers or sold to slave traders. They were also eager to secure tribute from defeated enemies, who were willing to pay in order to avoid further attacks. Under the alafins Ojigi and Tegbesu, for example, the Oyo mounted a series of raids into the kingdom of Dahomey, which lay just to the west of Yorubaland. By the terms of an agreement signed in 1730, the Dahomeans agreed to pay an annual tribute consisting of 40 men, 40 women, 40 guns, and 400 loads of cowries and corals.

The Oyo used this tribute to obtain even more horses and weapons, increasing their already daunting military power. In this way, Oyo was able to become the dominant state of Yorubaland. A Dutch merchant named Willem Bosman, who visited the coastal regions at the end of

(Continued on page 41)

36

YORUBA SCULPTURE

Following in the great artistic tradition of their ancestors, the Yoruba of present-day Nigeria rank among the foremost artists of Africa. Often working in wood, they have modified the naturalistic (or lifelike) techniques of Ife in favor of a more symbolic and abstract style.

This wooden mask is worn by those participating in the gelede *festival, which is designed to combat the influence of witchcraft. Witches are often blamed for a host of misfortunes, such as epidemics of disease and the inability of women to become pregnant.*

A 19th-century wood carving representing twins. The Yoruba believe that twins possess unusual spiritual power; when twins die during infancy, their spirits are preserved in sculptures that are fed, washed, and clothed as though they were living children.

A Yoruba divination figure representing the god Ifa. The Yoruba employ the complex rituals of Ifa divination in order to understand the influence of the gods over human affairs.

This carving from a Yoruba shrine depicts a figure on horseback, holding a chicken and surrounded by a group of worshipers. In Yoruba belief, the god Oduduwa descended from heaven with a five-toed chicken, which created the earth by scattering sand upon the waters.

(Continued from page 36)

the 17th century, wrote that the very mention of the Oyo was enough to terrify the peoples of the area. By the end of the following century, the Oyo were alleged to have 100,000 men under arms, and their power had grown to legendary proportions. According to an English observer quoted by historian Basil Davidson,

> The Dahomey people (then tributary to Oyo) used to say that when the Oyo people want to go to war, their general "spreads the hide of a buffalo before the door of his tent and pitches a spear on the ground on each side of it. Between these spears the soldiers march until the multitude which pass over the hide have worn a hole in it. As soon as this happens, the general presumes that his forces are numerous enough to take the field." [The Dahomey people] may possibly exaggerate, but the Oyo are certainly a very populous, warlike and powerful nation.

From accounts like these, it might be supposed that Oyo resembled the ancient Greek city-state of Sparta, where the warrior reigned supreme, while Ife played the role of Athens, the home of culture and democracy. In some ways this analogy holds true, because Oyo could never replace Ife as the spiritual and artistic center of Yorubaland. But

A statue of a Yoruba bowman, dating from the 14th or 15th century. Bowmen and spearmen often dipped their weapons in poison that would make even minor wounds potentially fatal; as a precaution, some warriors had their front teeth extracted so that antidotes could be poured down their throats even if their teeth were clenched in agony.

41

Oyo was not a one-dimensional state. In addition to their conquests, the alafins and their subjects also left a remarkable legacy of political organization.

Chapter 5 | THE WORLD OF OYO

A statue of a royal palace attendant, created by a 16th-century Yoruba sculptor. As the power of Oyo grew, its government became increasingly complex, with a host of officials serving the alafin and performing various functions in the government.

By the 17th century, the alafin of Oyo commanded recognition as "the supreme head of all the kings and princes of the Yoruba nation," in the words of Samuel Johnson. (Johnson, a Western-educated African from Sierra Leone, served as a Christian missionary among the Yoruba during the 19th century and wrote a richly detailed history of Yorubaland.) The coronation of a new alafin was an extended national holiday for which the people of Oyo turned out in great numbers, wearing their finest clothing. The elaborate ceremonies took place over the course of 20 days, beginning at the royal tombs on the outskirts of Oyo Ile. At the tombs the new ruler offered sacrifices to the spirits of his ancestors and received their permission to wear the crown. Five days later, he proceeded to the shrine of Shango, the thunder god, and accepted the symbols of his office: the beaded crown of Oduduwa, the royal robes, a staff, and a string of costly beads known as the *ejigba*. After five more days, he proceeded to the shrine of Oranmiyan, Oyo's founder, where he took possession of the Sword of Justice, which was brought especially for the occasion from Ile Ife. After final sacrifices at the shrine of Ogun, the god of war, the new alafin was entitled to enter his palace compound through a specially made opening in the outer wall—after his death the opening would be closed up permanently.

Throughout most of Oyo's history, the crown passed to the alafin's eldest son, who bore the title *aremo* (crown prince) during his father's lifetime and often became a joint ruler. During the 19th century, this custom was changed because

43

44

several aremos were suspected of doing away with their fathers. As a result, the Yoruba adopted a law decreeing that any prince who shared the throne with his father was also obliged to die with him.

In addition to the aremo and the king's wives, the royal court was staffed by a host of prominent officials. Among the most important were the master of the horse, whose function was to die with the king and serve him in the other world; the chief diviner, who consulted

This beaded crown (ade) is of the type worn by the alafin of Oyo and other rulers tracing their ancestry to Oduduwa, the creator of human beings and the first Yoruba monarch. Traditionally, the alafin takes possession of his crown at the shrine of Shango, the thunder god.

the oracle of Ifa every fifth day; the 200 or more palace musicians; the *arokin*, the bards who recited the deeds of the king's ancestors and the history of Oyo; the palace surveyor, in charge of maintaining the royal compound; and the king's executioners and their assistants.

Many of the above titles were hereditary, and the families that held them formed an elite group comparable to the aristocracies of European monarchies. In addition to hereditary officers, the alafins (and other rulers in Africa and the Middle East) created another class of officials—the eunuchs. In Yorubaland, the eunuchs (known as *iwefa*) were men who had been purchased for the king as boys and castrated before they reached puberty. Eunuchs were highly valued and often rose to positions of great power in West African kingdoms. Because they could not have children of their own, the eunuchs would not try to promote their family interest at the expense of the state, and rulers often trusted them more than other members of the royal court. In Oyo, the eunuchs were essentially in charge of all the day-to-day operations of the court, including the supervision of the alafin's wives. Among them was an official charged with hearing all petitions made to the king. Another eunuch attended the alafin at every moment, within the palace or in public, and was treated with the same respect due the monarch. The eunuchs also had a distinctive mode of dress, wearing long, sleeveless robes.

A third class of royal officials was the *ilari*. Both men and women were eligible to become ilari, and at any given time there might be hundreds of these officials, according to the will of the alafin. The ilari were commanded to shave alternate sides of their head every five days, leaving only a patch of hair at the top of the skull that was grown long and often braided. Upon appointment, each of the ilari took a new name celebrating the power of the alafin—"Upholder of the World," "Do Not Oppose Him," and so on. According to Johnson, the "favored ones ride upon the tallest horses whenever the King goes out in public, forming his body guards; others are servants to these; but their chief work one and all is that of house repair year by year."

The ilari were never lacking work, because the alafin's palace—known as the *afin*—was a massive complex, measuring a square mile in total area. Surrounded by protective walls on all sides, the palace was actually a series of interconnected compounds, each grouped around an inner courtyard or gallery. Separated from the compounds were outlying buildings housing stables, armories, storehouses for food, workshops, and the temples of major gods, such as Oduduwa, Shango, and Ogun.

In addition to housing the ilari, the palace musicians, and members of the royal family, the afin included the compounds of various important female officials. Among these was the *iya oba*, the alafin's "official" mother. (If the alafin's natural mother was alive at the time of his coronation, she was asked to commit suicide—or "go to sleep," as Johnson puts it—so that the alafin would not have to humble himself to any human being.) Other high-ranking women included the *iya kere*, who was in charge of the royal treasures and acted as the head of the ilari; the *iya naso*, responsible for rituals surrounding Shango; the *iyalagbon*, mother to the crown prince; and the areorite, the alafin's personal attendant, whose duties included that of holding a silken parasol above the ruler's head when he sat on the throne.

Despite the exalted position (and great wealth) of the alafin, he did not enjoy absolute power in Oyo. Still honoring their original family style of government, the Yoruba had developed a form of

45

constitutional monarchy. In a constitutional monarchy, such as that practiced in present-day Great Britain, the monarch is the official head of state but cannot exercise power without the consent of a legislature or other decision-making body. In Oyo, the function of the legislature was exercised by a council called the Oyo Mesi, which consisted of Oyo's leading chiefs. All judicial rulings and laws were the work of the Oyo Mesi, though the decisions and laws were announced in the name of the alafin. Beginning in the 17th century the Oyo Mesi had the added responsibility of choosing the alafin's successor from among the members of the royal family.

The military power of the alafin was limited also. As Oyo grew more powerful, a council of 70 war chiefs, known as the Eso, took over the management of the armed forces. The Eso were directed by an official known as the *bashorun*, whose personal compound lay just outside the palace walls. Only the alafin could approve the beginning of a military campaign; but the decision to go to war was a complicated process, requiring consultation with religious leaders as well as military commanders. The alafin could not mobilize the army without the consent of the war chiefs and the bashorun,

so he did not really possess the power to wage war.

The power of the bashorun, on the other hand, sometimes went far beyond the traditional limits. Between 1754 and 1774, for example, the bashorun Gaha was the true ruler of Oyo, subjecting both the alafin and the Oyo Mesi to his will and collecting much of the tribute money that was usually paid to the alafin. In the account of Johnson, Gaha "lived to a good old age, and wielded his power ruthlessly. He was noted for having raised five kings to the throne, of whom he murdered four, and was himself murdered by the fifth." Despite his great power, however, Gaha was unable to institute a foreign war during his reign, because the constitutional power to do so still rested with the alafin; the alafins refused to give the order, despite the certainty of being killed by Gaha, and the war chiefs would not mobilize their troops without receiving an order from the alafin.

The effects of this sophisticated political system filtered down throughout society, thoroughly influencing the ordinary Yoruba, who went about daily tasks such as farming, weaving, leather working, and pottery making. The character of the people, formed by centuries of prosperity and orderly self-government, was immediately apparent to foreigners who gained access to Yorubaland during the 19th century. Hugh Clapperton, a British military officer who traveled through West Africa in the late 1820s, was struck by the abundant evidence of a deep-seated civilization among the Yoruba:

> Here . . . is the poor dog treated with respect, and made the companion of man; here he had collars around his neck of different colors, and ornamented with cowries, and sits by his master, and follows him in all his journeys and visits. . . . In no other country of Africa, that I have been in, is this faithful animal treated with common humanity. . . . I cannot omit bearing testimony to the singular and perhaps unprecedented fact, that we have already travelled sixty miles in eight days, with numerous and heavy baggage, and about ten different relays of carriers, without losing so much as the value of a shilling public or private; a circumstance evincing not only somewhat more than common honesty in the inhabitants, but a degree of subordination and regular government which could not have been supposed to exist among a people hitherto considered barbarians.

But even as Clapperton wrote these admiring sentences, pressures from within and without threatened to destroy everything the Yoruba had created.

This elaborately carved door from a Yoruba palace depicts scenes of life in the royal court. The typical Yoruba palace was a massive complex housing hundreds of officials and servants as well as the royal family.

47

Chapter 6 | THE EMPTY CALABASH

When Oyo attained the height of its power at the end of the 18th century, it was said to control 6,600 towns and villages throughout Yorubaland and neighboring Dahomey. In this manner, Oyo emulated such empires as Mali and Songhay, and it was subject to the same stresses that had brought those empires crashing down after a century or two of grandeur.

Naturally, many of Oyo's subjects resented the power of the alafins. But as long as Oyo maintained its powerful military forces, bolstered by its rich trade along the coast, there was little possibility of revolt. By the end of the 18th century, however, during the reign of Alafin Abiodun, the awesome effectiveness of Oyo's soldiery began to decline. The reasons for this are not clear. It is possible

A 19th-century sculpture of a Yoruba horseman. By the middle of the century, the Oyo empire had crumbled, and wars between competing groups threatened the survival of Yorubaland.

that Abiodun's power struggle against Gaha, the tyrannical bashorun, caused dissension within the ranks of the army commanders. In any event, Oyo's army suffered two serious defeats within a decade. The first came at the hands of Borgu in 1783, during Abiodun's otherwise successful reign. Following Abiodun's death in 1789, he was succeeded by Awole, a man of lesser ability. During Awole's second year on the throne, Oyo's forces suffered disastrous defeat, at the hands of Nupe. Thus history came full cycle as Oyo's former enemies once again gained the upper hand.

The leading war chiefs of Oyo now lost confidence in Awole's leadership. They sent him an empty calabash (a gourd commonly used as a bottle or dipper), a gesture indicating that they no longer

50

A group of African captives are marched to a seaport where they will be sold to European slave traders. The transatlantic slave trade enriched a handful of Yoruba rulers but ultimately sowed chaos and corruption throughout the land.

accepted his authority. Under a law adopted by the Yoruba during the 18th century, this formal rejection by the chiefs obliged Awole to commit suicide by taking poison. Before he performed this dire act, however, the alafin entered the main courtyard of his palace and pronounced a curse upon his rebellious followers. As Johnson has related the scene, Awole first shot an arrow to the north, the south, and the west, and then uttered the following words:

> My curse be on you for your disloyalty and disobedience, so let your children disobey you. If you send them on an errand, let them never return to bring you word again. To all the points I shot my arrows will you be carried as slaves. My curse will carry you to the sea and beyond the seas, slaves will rule over you, and you, their masters, will become slaves.

Awole's curse was being fulfilled even as he took his life. The Atlantic slave trade had been in full swing for almost 200 years, depriving West Africa of many healthy men and women, who were now condemned to servitude in the Americas. Yoruba chiefs were able to gain great wealth by trading slaves to the Europeans, and their new status put them in direct competition with the alafins of

Oyo. In addition, Fulani Muslims were waging a successful war against the Hausa states directly to the north and were pressing into the northern regions of Yorubaland, determined to extend the influence of Islam. The Fulani "holy war" also disrupted the horse trade; as Oyo's cavalry declined, so did its ability to control Yorubaland.

One by one, the towns formerly under Oyo's control broke away, and the Dahomeans ceased to pay tribute to the alafin. Oyo sent forces to many regions in an attempt to put down these rebellions, but the troops were rarely successful. The defeated soldiers, upon learning that their homes in the north had been destroyed by Fulani raiders, often severed their ties to Oyo and set out on their own, seeking to take captives whom they could sell to slave traders. These freewheeling mercenaries, known as *omo ogun*, or "war boys," became a dangerous and disruptive force in Yorubaland and further weakened the control of Oyo. The final blow fell in 1835, when Alafin Olewu was resoundingly defeated by the Fulani cavalry at the Battle of Ilorin. After the defeat, the citizens of Oyo Ile fled south out of the war zone, and the once-glorious city lay abandoned. William H. Clarke, a Christian missionary who traveled in Yorubaland during the 1850s, reflected sadly upon the ruins he encountered:

> Within a few short days, that which was once powerful and flourishing, was now flowing with blood, covered with sackcloth, bathed in tears; and the farms in a state of cultivation were left to the wild beasts and the over-powering growth of weeds and grass. . . . Such scenes as these were too much for a man to see and bear without being moved to pity if not to tears.

Though a new Oyo was later built at a site some 70 miles to the west, the Oyo empire would never rise again. The "war boys" now reigned supreme. Robert Smith has described the years between the fall of Oyo and the end of the 19th century in the following terms:

> This was a time not merely of conflict but of political, social, and economic change, partly engendered by the wars and partly by the opening of the country to European influence on a large scale and in different forms. New states arose out of the wreckage of Oyo, and older states, previously overshadowed by Oyo, asserted their independence. Firearms, first the primitive muskets and then modern rifles, played an increasing part in the wars. . . . European slave traders, dealing through African middlemen,

51

A street scene in Lagos, Nigeria's largest city and main seaport. Town dwellers since time immemorial, the Yoruba make up the bulk of the population in Lagos and other leading Nigerian cities.

were gradually replaced by (or transformed into) the buyers of palm oil and other produce of the interior. Christian missionaries blazed a trail inland . . . setting up a chain of stations designed to reach into the Muslim north.

In this time of turmoil, the centers of power in Yorubaland shifted to the south, where the forests provided a barrier against the marauding Fulani cavalry operating out of Ilorin. For the rest of the 19th century, the southern states of Ibadan, Abeokuta, and Ijaye competed for supremacy. As a result, the life of the Yoruba communities was frequently disrupted by warfare, the effects of which were aggravated by raids from Dahomey to the west and Benin to the east. By midcentury, the situation was further complicated by the growing presence of the British, who took possession of the port city of Lagos in 1852 and steadily expanded their influence.

The death knell for Yoruba independence sounded in 1878 with the outbreak of the Sixteen Years' War, which pitted the Fulani and a coalition of Yoruba states against Ibadan. Despite an early victory by Ibadan at the Battle of Irikun in 1878—known in Yoruba as the "rush to the water" because of the mass drowning of fleeing Fulani troops in the River Otin—the war dragged on indecisively year after year. Christian missionaries, including the historian Samuel Johnson, made strenuous efforts to bring about peace between the warring kingdoms. A cease-fire finally took effect in 1886, ending all the fighting except for the war between Ibadan and the Fulani state of Ilorin. But this was, in any case, only a temporary respite for the Yoruba.

During 1884 and 1885, the major European powers had convened in Berlin, Germany, to devise a formula for dividing up Africa into colonies. Yorubaland had been coveted by the French as well as the British, and the Berlin delegates agreed that Britain had rights to the territory—provided that the British were able to occupy it. After British forces defeated the Ijebu in 1892 in a fierce battle along the Yemoji River, they negotiated a series of agreements with the Yoruba states, by which the exhausted and divided Africans agreed to accept British rule. In 1893, both the Sixteen Years' War and the independence of Yorubaland came to an end.

Under British rule, Yorubaland was incorporated into the larger colony of Nigeria, which included Hausaland, Igboland, and Borno. The British believed that the system of "indirect rule" was the best way to control their African possessions. They attempted to exercise authority through the traditional chiefs of the Yoruba communities and tried to turn the clock back by making Oyo the dominant power of Yorubaland. This policy aroused bitter opposition in Yorubaland. The most traditional Yoruba wanted to reinstate the old family style of government rather than submit to the power of Oyo once again. At the other end of the spectrum, Yoruba who had been educated by Christian missionaries demanded the same political freedoms enjoyed by citizens of Western industrial nations. Both groups were frequently at odds with the British government.

Despite the conflicts and humiliations of the colonial period, the Yoruba's perseverance produced a number of long-term benefits, as Robert Smith has indicated:

> Shielded by foreign arms and power from the Dahomeans . . . and the Fulani, and forbidden to engage in their own internccinc wars, the Yoruba were free to discover a cultural unity within the new political unity imposed upon them, and in a few years were invited to share in an even wider identification as Nigerians, fellow-citizens with the Hausa, Kanuri, Igbo, Ijo, Edo, and the rest of Nigeria's many different peoples. Within a half-century this was to engender among the educated a sense of belonging to a nation, the most populous and one of the most important in Africa.

When Nigeria achieved its independence in 1960, the Yoruba, 10 million strong, emerged as the third-largest of the new nation's 250 ethnic groups, exceeded only by the Hausa and the Igbo. The Yoruba continue to be town-dwellers, with the result that Nigeria's 10 largest

53

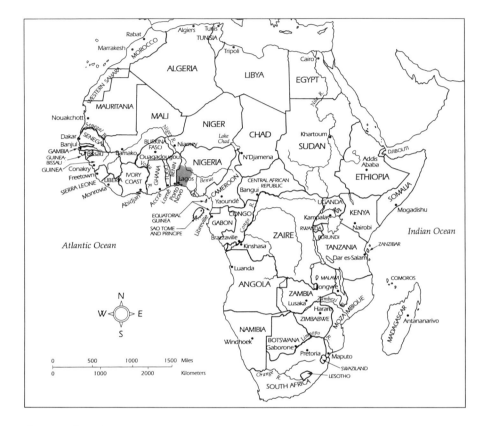

A map of contemporary Africa, with the shaded area indicating the territory of Yorubaland in southern Nigeria.

ria's former capital, in size and wealth.

Because their ancient practices were never seriously disrupted by colonialism, the Yoruba have maintained many of their ancestral traditions. Large portions of their towns are still organized into compounds based on descent lines, while newer sections are completely modern, featuring detached houses and all the conveniences of 20th-century cities. As J. S. Eades has written in his book *The Yoruba Today*, "Elders are still given siderable respect and deference in public, and men with higher levels of education, well established in public life, will still prostrate before them."

Most of the Yoruba continue to practice traditional occupations such as farming, weaving, dyeing, and leatherwork and are also highly skilled as traders. Moreover, the artistic traditions of the Yoruba are as powerful as ever. Many of Africa's leading artists—in sculpture, textiles, and music—are Yoruba, and as a whole, the Yoruba produce a greater number of artworks than any other African people.

The Yoruba have made their presence felt not only in Africa but throughout the world. Beginning in the 16th century, Yoruba captives who were transported as slaves to the Americas carried their tradi-

cities are predominantly Yoruba. Ife, the spiritual center of the Yoruba nation, is now a thriving city of more than 200,000 people and the home of Nigeria's largest university; an extensive museum displays the great bronzes of Ife. New Oyo has never recaptured the grandeur of Oyo Ile, but Ibadan, the capital of Oyo State, is a thriving metropolis of more than 1 million people, second only to Lagos, Nige-

54

tions with them. As a result, Yoruba religious beliefs have remained vibrantly alive in such nations as Brazil and Cuba. In Puerto Rico, Yoruba beliefs have combined with Roman Catholic observances to form the religion of Santería. Throughout the Americas, diviners still mediate between worshipers and the oracle of Ifa, though they often do so through a more simplified procedure known as "16 cowries," in which small white cowrie shells are used in place of palm nuts and in which there are fewer possible combinations and fewer verses to be memorized by the babalawo.

The Yoruba worldview has thus extended far beyond Africa, and its influence has not been limited to peoples of black African ancestry. Afolabi Epega, a fifth-generation Nigerian babalawo, has advanced a universal interpretation of the Yoruba faith: "Ifa is not a black religion it is an African religion originating from Ile Ife. . . . Oosanla, or Obatala as he is better known in the West, one of our more important orisa, was white. Ifa teaches that people of all colors were born into the earth from Ile Ife. . . . Ifa teaches integrating with the world in every aspect. To segregate any part is to stray from the path." Indeed, one of the babalawo's leading pupils is Philip John Neimark, a white American businessman who was introduced to Yoruba religion in Miami, Florida, in 1974. In his book *The Way of the Orisa*, Neimark explains that Ifa provided him with the spiritual satisfaction that his life had previously lacked; in the ensuing years, he himself became a leading babalawo under the name Fagbamila and introduced many more Americans to Yoruba religious beliefs. In this and many other ways, the ancient traditions of one of the world's great civilizations remain as vibrantly alive as they were 1,000 years ago in the sacred groves of the dense West African forest.

55

CHRONOLOGY

4th century A.D.	Yoruba people begin to settle in the West African forest belt, in what is now southwestern Nigeria; Ile Ife emerges as the spiritual center of Yorubaland; Yoruba begin to trade with people living in the savanna to the north
c. 600	Chiefs and kings emerge among the Yoruba as population increases and society becomes more complex
c. 1300	New rulers, possibly immigrants from Hausaland, establish themselves in Ile Ife
12th–14th centuries	Artists of Ife produce terra-cotta sculptures for use in royal burial ceremonies
14th–15th centuries	Artists of Ife produce bronze masterpieces, using lost-wax method
late 16th century	Oyo begins to emerge as the dominant state of Yorubaland after Alafin Orompoto builds up cavalry forces
17th century	Alafins Obalokun and Ajagbo lead Oyo's forces in conquests of neighboring states; Oyo gains control of seaport of Ajase and begins to trade with Europeans; transatlantic slave trade exerts a powerful influence on West African societies
1730	Rulers of Dahomey agree to pay annual tribute to Oyo

1754–74	Bashorun (army commander) Gaha controls the government of Oyo, murdering four alafins who oppose him; Oyo attains the height of its power
1774	Alafin Abiodun overthrows Gaha; orderly government returns to Oyo, but power of its armies begins to decline
1783	Oyo suffers military defeat at the hands of Borgu
c. 1796	Oyo's war chiefs depose Alafin Awole, who lays a curse upon his people before committing suicide
early 19th century	Fulani Muslims launch "holy war" in Hausaland and press into northern Yorubaland; more and more subject states break away from Oyo
1835	Fulani defeat Oyo's forces at the Battle of Ilorin; Oyo Ile is destroyed; Yorubaland plunged into chaos as states of Ibadan, Abeokuta, and Ijaye compete for supremacy
1878–93	Sixteen Years' War waged between Ibadan and other Yoruba states; war ends with British occupation of Yorubaland
1893–1960	Yorubaland forms part of British colony of Nigeria
1960	Nigeria achieves independence; Yoruba represent the new nation's third-largest ethnic group and form the core of the population in Nigeria's major cities

FURTHER READING

Ajayi, J. F. A., and R. Smith. *Yoruba Warfare in the 19th Century.* Cambridge: Cambridge University Press, 1971.

Bascom, W. R. *Ifa Divination: Communication Between Gods and Men in West Africa.* Bloomington: Indiana University Press, 1969.

————. *16 Cowries: Yoruba in Africa and the New World.* Bloomington: Indiana University Press, 1980.

Clarke, W. H. *Travels and Explorations in Yorubaland, 1854–1858.* Edited by J. A. Atanda. Ibadan: Ibadan University Press, 1972.

Connah, Graham. *African Civilizations.* Cambridge: Cambridge University Press, 1987.

Davidson, Basil. *Africa in History.* Rev. ed. New York: Collier, 1991.

————. *The African Genius.* Boston: Little, Brown, 1969.

Davidson, Basil, with F. K. Buah and the Advice of J. F. A. Ajayi. *A History of West Africa, 1000–1800.* New rev. ed. London: Longmans, 1977.

Eades, J. S. *The Yoruba Today.* Cambridge: Cambridge University Press, 1980.

Hull, Richard W. *African Cities and Towns Before the European Conquest.* New York: Norton, 1976.

Johnson, Samuel. *The History of the Yorubas from the Earliest Times to the Beginning of the British Protectorate.* 1921. Reprint. New York: Negro University Press, 1969.

Lawson, Thomas. *Religions of Africa*. New York: Harper & Row, 1984.

McEvedy, Colin. *The Penguin Atlas of African History*. New York: Penguin, 1980.

Neimark, Philip John. *The Way of the Orisa*. San Francisco: HarperSanFrancisco, 1993.

Ojo, G. J. A. *Yoruba Palaces*. London: University of London Press, 1966.

Oliver, Roland, and Brian M. Fagan. *Africa in the Iron Age*. Cambridge: Cambridge University Press, 1975.

Park, Mungo. *Travels in the Interior Districts of Africa*. 1799. Reprint. New York: Arno Press / New York Times, 1971.

Shaw, Thurstan. *Nigeria: Its Archaeology and Early History*. London: Thames and Hudson, 1978.

Smith, Robert S. "Yoruba Armament." *Journal of African History* 7 (1967): 87–106.

———. *Kingdoms of the Yoruba*. 3rd ed. Madison: University of Wisconsin Press, 1988.

———. *Warfare and Diplomacy in Pre-Colonial West Africa*. 2nd ed. Madison: University of Wisconsin Press, 1989.

UNESCO General History of Africa. 8 vols. Berkeley: University of California Press, 1980–93.

Webster, J. B., and A. A. Boahen, with M. Tidy. *The Revolutionary Years: West Africa Since 1800*. New ed. London: Longman, 1980.

Willett, Frank. "Ife and Its Archaeology." *Journal of African History* 1 (1960): 231–48.

———. *Ife in the History of West African Sculpture*. London: Thames and Hudson, 1967.

GLOSSARY

alafin   title borne by the ruler of Oyo; the most powerful monarch in Yorubaland between the 16th and 19th centuries

archaeology   the study of the physical remains of past human societies

babalawo   ("father of secret things" in Yoruba) a Yoruba priest who communicates with Ifa, the god of divination, and reveals individual destinies

bale   the elder of a Yoruba clan or descent line; also known as *oloro ebi*

bashorun   the commander of Oyo's armies

bronze   an alloy (combination of metals) of copper and tin; used by the artists of Ife to create life-size sculptures of human heads

clan   a social group united by descent from a common ancestor; also known as a descent line

constitutional monarchy   a system of government in which the monarch is the official head of state but shares power with a council or legislative body

divination   the art of foretelling future events or discovering hidden knowledge, as practiced by Yoruba babalawos

ebi   ("family" in Yoruba) the principle of government by which all the states of Yorubaland were supposed to be equal members of the Yoruba family

lost-wax method   the intricate bronze-casting technique employed by the Yoruba sculptors of Ife

oni   the title borne by the ruler of Ife; the oni of Ife is regarded as the spiritual leader of the Yoruba people

orisa   the more than 400 gods and goddesses of the Yoruba religion

Oyo Mesi   the council of ministers that governed Oyo in concert with the alafin

terra-cotta   a form of clay that develops a lasting hardness when heated in a fire; used as a medium by many West African sculptors and potters

tsetse fly   an insect that lives in the West African forest belt and transmits a deadly disease commonly known as sleeping sickness

INDEX

63

PHILIP KOSLOW earned his B.A. and M.A. degrees from New York University and went on to teach and conduct research at Oxford University, where his interest in medieval European and African history was awakened. The editor of numerous volumes for young adults, he is also the author of *El Cid* in the Chelsea House HISPANICS OF ACHIEVEMENT series and of *Centuries of Greatness: The West African Kingdoms, 750–1900* in Chelsea House's MILESTONES IN BLACK AMERICAN HISTORY series.

PICTURE CREDITS